The Unive... Is Rooting for You!

Written/Art Directed by:

Dan Sadlowski

Illustrated/Watercolors by:

Allison Pierce

Digital Editing/Mastering by:

Emily Gabriel

Watercolor Guest Artist:

Samantha Sadlowski

"Look at that little boy over there.

Nobody next to him.

Nobody even cares.

You can barely see him in that big ol' sweater of his.

He looks like a Little... Lump."

Author's Note

The Universe Is Rooting for You was created to remind us to take the time to appreciate the natural world around us. Nature is so awe-inspiring and loves us in so many ways. Encourage your children, students, family members, friends, and yourself to connect with nature. Explore it. Go on new adventures. Open your imagination, heart, and mind. Look around, who knows what you may find.

Special thank you to: My family, friends, students, and nature.
You are AWE-MAZING! Thank you for always rooting for me.
To my sister Emily for your endless kindness, creativity, and dedication.
My wife Samantha for your amazing art and fun-loving encouragement.
To Allison for your hard work and heartfelt illustrations.

For: Anyone who has ever felt sad and alone like the Little Lump.
Remember, you are not alone. The universe is rooting for you!

Off on a **STUMP** sat a sad **Little Lump**.

The **UNIVERSE** shouted.

"Um, yesss??"
said the **Little Lump** .

Then the

UNIVERSE

had something
to say...

" Don't fret, my **Little Lump** .
Even when you're down in the dumps,
the **EARTH** rumbles, bumbles, and bumps.
For it does NOT want to see you that way.

When it **RAINS**,
it's not to bring you down
but to wash away your frown.

It wishes to
comfort you.

The **FLOWERS** speak,

"You are
more beautiful
than you know."

"Let's help
eachother
grow."

The **TREES** teach you to be strong and stand tall.

The
LEAVES
show
you
it's
Ok
to
fall.

The bright **SUN** wants to shine like you do!

The **MOUNTAINS** shout from the mountaintops,
"GO, Little Lump,

GO, Little Lump,

GO!!"

The **WIND** yearns to soar with you!

The OCEAN waves come crashing back to be with you.

And every once in a while, the **MOON** will try to copy your smile.

The UNIVERSE is rooting for you, Little Lump, and now you know.

These are just a few
things that love you so.

"Wow, it's true!"
thought the **Little Lump**.

"Everything in the **UNIVERSE**
is rooting for me and has my back.

Now, it's my turn to take care of the entire **UNIVERSE** and *give back*."

Simple ways YOU can connect with NATURE and give back like the Little Lump !

- Plant a **tree**.

- Start a **garden**.

- Stop and smell the **roses**.

- Find something in **nature** that is **beautiful** to **you**.

- **Write or draw**: 3 things in the **universe** that are **rooting for you**.

- Play outside in your **bare feet**.

- Hike a **mountain**.

- Organize a **beach** clean up.

- Share the **Little Lump's story**!

BONUS PAGES

The **Little Lump** spent time connecting with **NATURE**:

Playing outside barefoot, climbing **TREES**, and befriending many **FLOWERS**.

In return, the UNIVERSE gave the Little Lump AWE-MAZING SUPERPOWERS!

⭐ <u>The Little Lump's powers:</u>
The abilty to make trees and plants multiply, move, and grow at super speeds.

The Little Lump set out to use his superpowers to protect and defend nature in hopes to save the universe.

Check us out at:

findingbrooklyn-book.com
facebook.com/theuniverseisrootingforyou
instagram.com/thenextgreatsuperhero

#gofindingbrooklyn
#golittlelump

We'd love to hear from you!

Library of Congress Number 2019915453
ISBN 978-0-9978618-1-5
Copyright © 2019 by Dan Sadlowski
Printed in the U.S.A.